new words {press}
New York, NY
www.newwordspress.com

new words {press} is a sponsored non-profit poetry press dedicated to elevating emerging and established trans* and gender-expansive poetic voices, building community, and sharing knowledge.

ISBN: 978-1-968528-00-3

Cover art by Rafael Santiago
Cover layout by brooklyn baggett
Editorial Support by Ira Silverberg
Typesetting by brooklyn baggett
Font: Bakersville and Source Sans Variable

Printed in the United States of America

The Tenderness of Glass

poems

Jodi Lin

new words {press}

A TRANS* & GENDER-EXPANSIVE POETRY PRESS

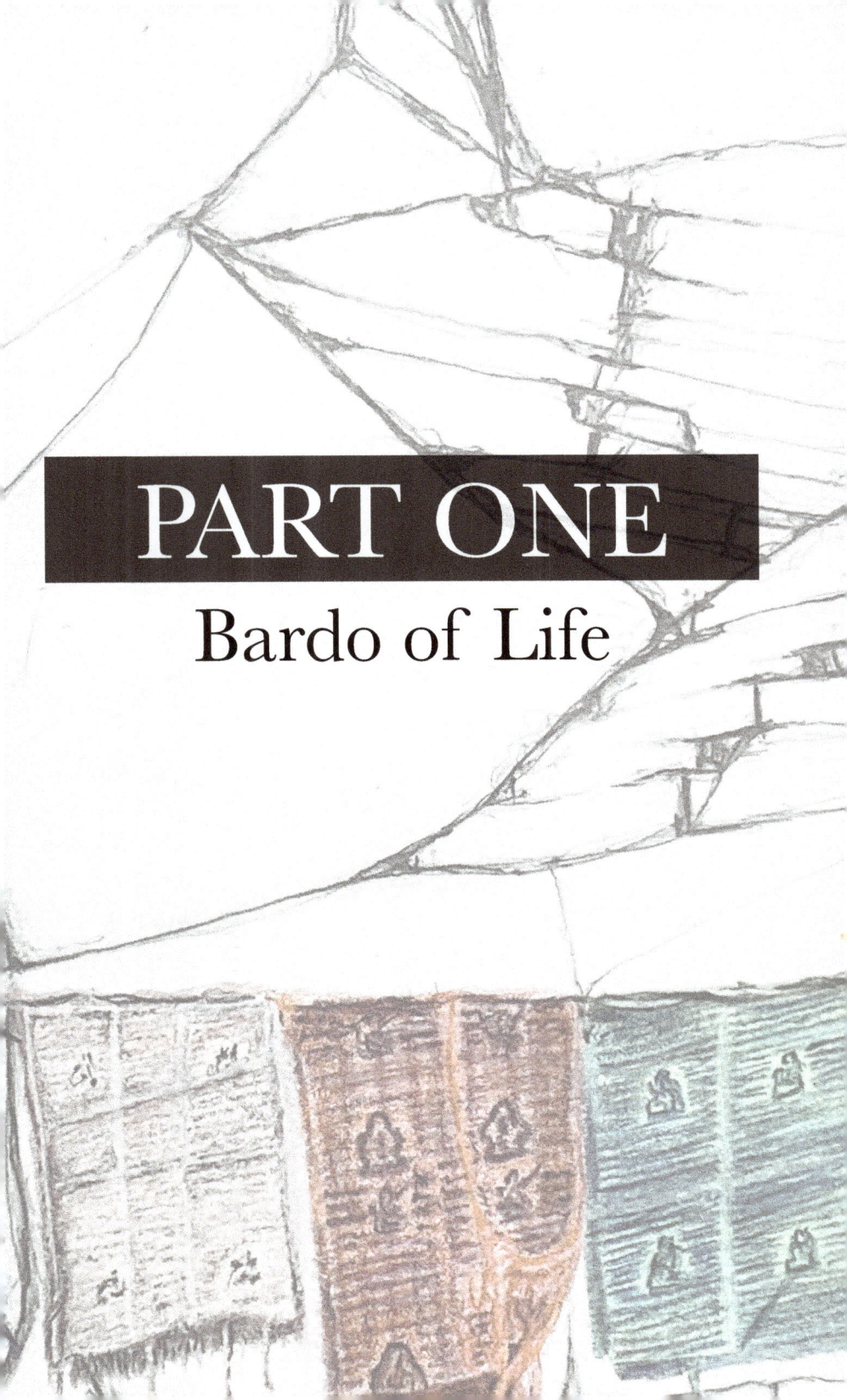

PART ONE

Bardo of Life

I.I

Goddess! I call to you, and you intervene!
Wrathfully, you come, radiant and pure, blue bodied—
Emanating pure light through your skin, your soul!
Your blue body, again! Like the brave body you chose
When you ascended the underworld!

Protectress! Riding the night sky!
I call to you, and you intervene! Have mercy on us!
I petition you to protect the dharma once again.
Ride the night sky on your horse, wrapped in
The now sacred skins of your only son.

Goddess of wrath! Queen Goddess Divine!
Like a holy terror, riding the night sky! Your son's
Tender skull in one hand, your holy scepter in the other.
His brains and blood, still warm in your fearsome grip!
Your power leads you through the underworld and back!

Goddess! Palden Lhamo! Choose me!
Your blue skin turned clear light!
Choose me, as I choose you!
Let me be you, lifetime to life, cross with me.
Goddess incarnate, let me be life!

I.II

They/them
Now/then
Missing/found.
One breath in
Another out.
In and out.

        Don't know when it began
        But suddenly it was over.

Why do all queers
Have so many tattoos
And smoke so many cigarettes?

        I wanted to be straight

        And then I met with fate

        And it was over
        And over
        And over.

I.III

In the Asia of the ancients
Tribal women tattoo each other
To keep from being stolen for sex.

I have four tattoos.

Each one acquired within the year that I fell in love.

A flame lotus.
     A peacock feather.
          Naryana.
          A blue bodied moth with evil eyes for wings.

Each one a map of my freedom.

Each one for you.

I.IV

He caught fish with his feet
        In the familial waters.

           The island he would share with me
                   Even if I never asked.
                       With strong leathery hands

                       He built elaborate houses in trees.
               I was too small to climb there
        But too big to carry up.

  So the stilted houses were mine
          To inherit—

          When I was big enough
              Fearless enough

                  To climb
               With bare feet
            And sun kissed
          Golden skin
       Like him

     To that sweet shelter
    Nestled there
  Misplaced
And regal
    In a suburban backyard tree.

I.V

She
She told me I was thin skinned
She

With crooked fingers
She
Bristles on a hairbrush

Pain metal

Combing thin skin
From my tender scalp.

There in the shower
Naked and small
I balanced on a wobbly foot stool
The stool
To make the reach easier on her back
As the hot water ran over me.

She pressed on harder
She.

The water
Salty now
She.

Was it the tears
Was it the sea
Was it the blood that rose up from my heart to the bristles

Pain metal

Brushing my innocence
With venom hands
From her venom heart.
She

Thin skin torn
Tender

From this little girl
Whose little mouth
Told the lie
That was the truth
That ruined
The family
Her family
Name.

I.VI

The abduction happened nightly. A force would pull me through the ceiling. Rape me in the sky, then return my ravaged little body to the bed. What happened next warms my heart. A white cat, and the seven-year-old me was revived. I'd follow the cat from the door to the hall, then to the last shelf of my father's bookcase. I was small enough to fit. It happened so often that my mother knew to find me there in the morning.

I.VII

I was a child and I wore red lipstick to bed.

I. VIII

You said you liked it.
You said you liked him.
He spit on me down there
As he spoke.
I don't remember what hurt worse.
The spit.
The cream.
Big fingers.
Big tongue.
He put the boy on top of me
As he masturbated and watched.
What hurt
I don't remember.
What hurt worse.

I.IX

Last night he was kissing me in my bed, I told her. We fell silent, held together in that dark space. Rocketed into the pain place of my mind. I was there again last night. In my body, his on top of mine. Kissing and kissing me until I woke. Stolen.

I.X

I had finished packing my last bag when my karma urged me to lay down one last time. His desperate eyes emerged through the crack of the half open door. We weren't allowed to close our bedroom doors because they were always watching; waiting and watching. Standing there in his underwear and undershirt, he wanted in, like a child begging for the comfort of his parents' bed. Can I, he asked, as our roles reversed. I rolled over in the bed to face away, disgusted by his immense need for me. Not seeing my face, he took this as an invitation to get under my mother's favorite peach colored duvet. It was a few months after my high school graduation day. I would be leaving in a few hours, for good I hoped, a coast away from this pain place that I called home. He got into my bed and with a jolt lifetimes pulsed through my body. Has this been happening my whole life, I thought. Has this been happening this whole life. Get out I screamed. Get out!

I.XI

Running from falling towers revived memories I had tried to drown and murder with liquor. From near death, a new consciousness emerged. Once comfortable in my ignorance of intoxicants, I was shocked when the fog of rebirth began to lift and fade. No amount of self-destruction could keep the memories down anymore. I was 26 when I returned. Home was not exactly how I left it. Stuffed animals were placed on the bed pillows where there were never any. That night I lay beneath the peach duvet to find that I wasn't alone again. I closed my eyes to sleep, inhaling deeply, hoping that the stillness of sleep could erase what I had always known. The half dream became a waking nightmare that I could feel and smell. The room was lit bright pink. I was high and couldn't get down. A force pulled me through the ceiling again, like it did when I was a child. This time it was him. His face where there hadn't ever been one.

I.XII

I got the voice message after work that day. He was dying and his sister wanted me there. It had been nine years. Nine years of peace. Nine years of bitter sweet bliss. Liver failure. Cirrhosis. Hepatitis C. Kidney failure. Gout. Sepsis. A weak heart from where they opened him. I want to say that I felt nothing for him but that's not true. My body remembered and I hurt. The pain pulled me through the ceiling and raped me in the sky. I saw his alien face. Red eyes like a starved street rat hungry for my pain. I arrived to the hospital room. Although he was grey with death I could see him. His face. Pulling me through the ceiling and raping me in the sky. I was high and the room was pink and my ravaged little body returned. There in the hospital room. I saw his face for what felt like the first time. Grey with death and to my delight I knew that it was almost over. Almost. Was I sick or was it him. It was him.

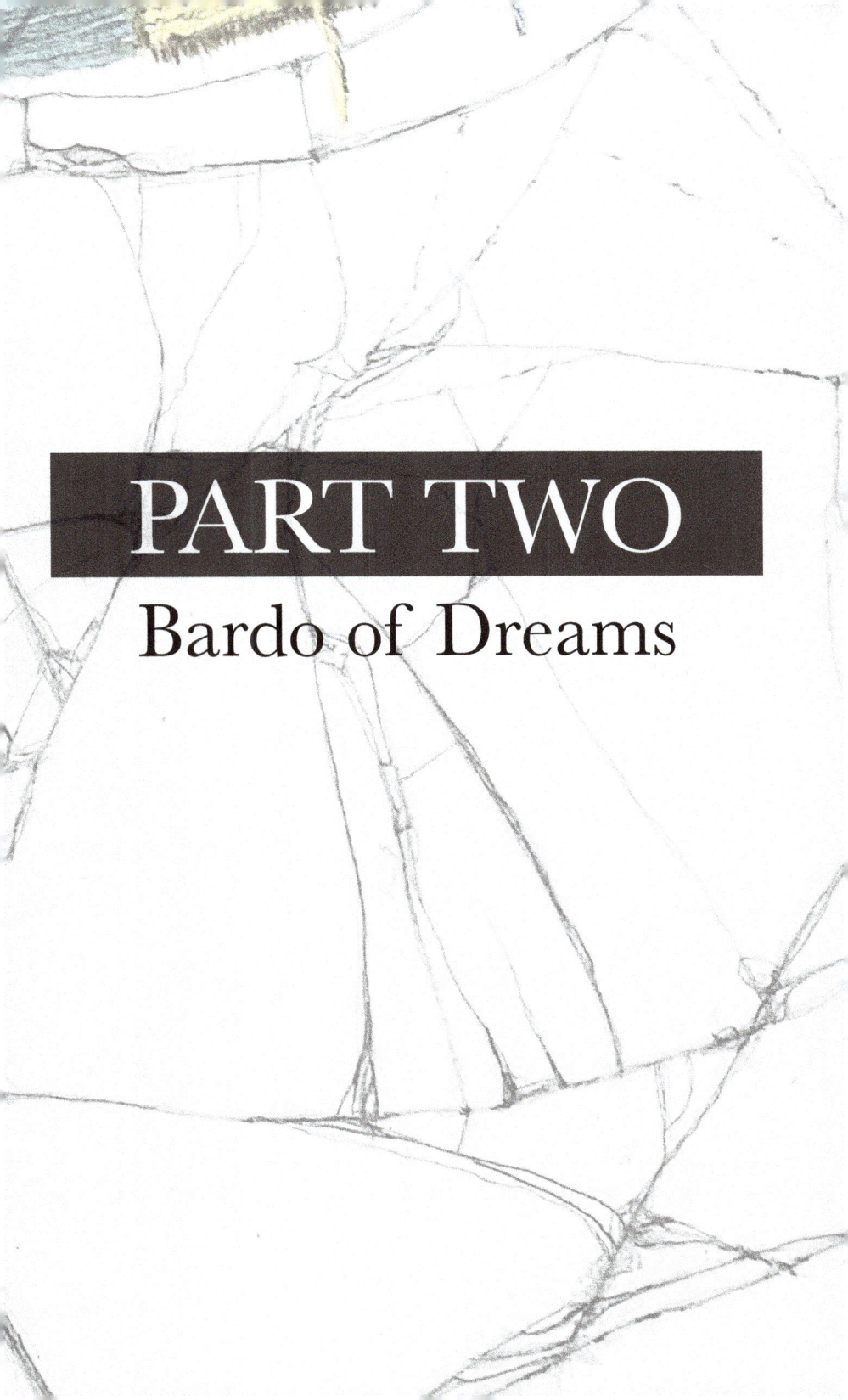

PART TWO

Bardo of Dreams

Fight, Goddess, fight! Goddess, take flight!
Goddess, be brave! He couldn't be saved!
The supreme sacrifice! My only son!
Heir to the land without Buddhism,
I saved the dharma! This is my karma!

Now, to the underworld! The gift is the curse!
My power is my true love devotion to this earth!
Crossing through brings me wealth! Crossing through brings me fame!
I saved the dharma and am deified! Adorned with sacred love!
Oh Siddhartha! Oh glorious, Siddhartha! Hear my prayer!

Fight, Goddess, fight! Goddess, take flight!
Goddess, be brave! He couldn't be saved!
The supreme sacrifice! My only son!
Heir to the land without Buddhism,
I saved the dharma! This is my karma!

Queen Goddess Divine!

Namaste soha!
Namaste soha!
Namaste soha!

I want to remember every detail but my royal heart won't give it all back to me. I called the police and told them there were three human skulls under my bed. They came with the hazardous materials truck, expecting bodies, blood and carnage. Finding no skulls the line of questioning went something like this— Do you know what day it is, Miss? Do you know where you are? Do you know who the president is? When was the last time that you ate? When was the last time that you slept? Did somebody hurt you? Or try to hurt you? Something like this. I don't know what I said. I didn't pass the test. They asked me to close my apartment window. They suggested I grab my coat. They suggested I grab my keys. An ID. I put on my fanciest coat with my fanciest hat. Handed my keys, phone, and ID to an officer as though she worked for me. And…I was escorted to an ambulance. A technician took my vitals and gave me the peanut butter and jelly sandwich that broke the power of my renunciate austerity, my forty day almond milk fast. He assured me that I didn't need to worry. I was going somewhere safe. I wrote a letter that got the president shot. Could you take me to court? You have to show up for court or you'll be in even more trouble than you were in the first place. And I think I need a lawyer? There's no court today, Miss. And President Obama is alive and well as far as I know. In fact, the first family just adopted a dog. Do you know what day it is? Oh god, I thought, these questions again. But I realized I didn't know the answer.

II.III

I grew up thinking people could fly. The night I wound up in the
hospital, the evil force, disguised as the voice of my ancestors,
told me to jump out of the window. I was so blessed I could fly
it told me. In that moment I felt an invisible wall, like tender
glass, hold space between me and the dawn sky. Could the
light of my spirit, my nature of mind— could it overpower the
negative manifestations who talk to me, who speak to me in my
own voice. The answer I know now is yes but not without
cause. Not without effect. I spent forty days in the mind prison
that is Bellevue. The holy queen's buddha nature challenged by
illusion.

II.IV

I lay in my hospital bed waiting for my roommates to fall asleep.
So I could touch myself so quietly and cum. One of the nurses
kept saying chinky chinky chinky. Another patient called me
selfish for not asking my friends to sneak me cigarettes. She
said doing that one thing would bring so many people
happiness. I refused she said. The doctors wanted me to make
friends there. Selfish for not wanting to, although a cigarette
would taste so good.

II.V

The rec room roared with a special kind of over medicated
excitement. Who was going to win? It really didn't matter. None
of us lunatics had even seen any of the movies. 2010 was my
year. Me in my fancy coat and hat. Walking the red carpet. I
would have raced in at the last minute. Only losers arrive early.
My fancy coat. My fancy hat. You could be my date but we
haven't met yet.

II.VI

Good behavior meant I could go to the roof. I would be lying if I
said I didn't think about jumping again. I longed for the other
side of the gates and beyond. The manhattan view was just too
beautiful. I wanted to forgive you. I wanted to be close. But I
didn't know you yet. Not in this life.

II.VII

I gained thirty-three pounds in the hospital. The almond milk fasts kept me powerful. I was to cleanse the city of evil spirits, to prove my mind power. Three mirrors facing one another— Srila Prahbupad chanting the Maha Mantra and a very old TV set that would pull the dark spirits to the other side. The exorcisms were a loving service I provided all day and all night, taking breaks to go the restaurant where I worked as a server. Me, the reincarnation of the pure and holy queen goddess, the daughter of the Dalai Lama from a past life. Karma from the last life and the life before that and the life before that. Centuries strong. The ancestors said no one would understand until I ascend the throne in this life. I lost faith too. And that's how I wound up here. Drinking ensure. Medication put my body in a starved survival state. A hungry ghost, eating pudding and peanut butter and jelly sandwiches.

II.VIII

Once in the morning. Once in the afternoon. Once at night. And then in the morning again. To dull the pain of the memories too big to conquer. Even in my hospital bed. Even in the room I share with three others. I touch myself and I dull the pain and pray that no one else hears me gasp.

II.IX

Karma is constantly changing. I missed my chance to be the sacred queen. I was scared. In a split second the fear changed my fate. Perhaps the consequence was life. Because if it were true that I could fly I'd be up in the sky soaring with you. And now I suffer in that funny in-between place. Grounded like a punishment. Grounded. Time out. I've fallen out of love with life.

PART THREE

Bardo of Meditation

III.I

I could hear the crack of the ice from where I stood on the rocks. A symphony of broken ice, like shards of glass rubbing close together, a song yet to be written. Not that I have an ear for music. It was M. I was thinking of M and missing him. I was thinking about one of the many conversations we had. It was his birthday he told me. Deep in winter after a heavy snowfall, he said, as we strolled and talked where the path meets the water along the brooklyn bridge park. He had come to the water to die. Too afraid to jump he lay down in the snow, spread out like a snow angel. What does fallen snow sound like he thought. And as he lay there listening, he could hear the sound of crashing ice, the hudson river frozen over. Aw baby I said. Sad that he wanted to die. But so in love with the way he saw the world. I was mesmerized at the time or was it death. Love and death. I had come here in winter looking for him. The memory of him and the emotion I felt the night we strolled. I wanted to forgive him. I wanted to be close again.

III.II

.....

to keep me honest
i brought a friend
to our first date

i feel it in my core
long before the act

a salty taste
a hunger

far back in my throat
where one day i know i'll find it

tip for tip

i touch it

with the most sensitive
part of my mouth
and let it water

like salty blood
from a salty wound

        for you

           i felt

       nothing

           and i knew

       that

           i loved you.

.....

III.III

that first kiss
lips pressed close
tongue tickles

. . . . .

breathing you
in sweet gasps
expanding warmth

. . . . .

fingers

then hands

then heart

. . . . .

pulling in
pulling close
then in again

closer still

i want to

.....

push you around

in a play stroller
like the way
small children
proudly do

.....

you're my babydoll
       wrapped in warm
             and fuzzy feelings

.....

me all grown up

.....

watching you
       strolling with you

.....

through a dreamland of
unicorns and rainbows.

III. V

i wrote this for you on the train:

you were a girl with the smallest features

.....

blue grey eyes

that blend sweetly with   the brown of your skin

.....

talking eyes   eyes that speak

.....

my heart

III.VI

.....

invisible

the space
between
two halves
pushed and pulled
into nothing.

a pause a breath a moment

invisible.

i wait
hold it in
till it breaks.

i wait
and you appear.

and nothing
is the something
i wait for.

III.VII

I just wanted to see you, you said. My fractured heart became whole. We sat in my tiny apartment. Your face bled from a scratch. Your funny fingers that I loved so much made a funny mark on your face that I loved so much. I crossed my legs and you noticed. Then I remembered that no one had seen you with your shirt off in ten years. Breasts that only your binder could hide. I love your breasts even if you don't, I thought. I love your breasts. I love your breasts and your blue grey eyes that held my tender heart together that day. We smoked cigarettes and talked about the nothing that was everything and I loved you again and again. For a moment I believed that you loved me too.

III. VIII

.....
.....
.....

I quit smoking the day
I got over you.
Nothing about me
Reminds me of you
Anymore.

III.IX

Folded over
Like the weakest branch of a tree
The leaves
Once heavy with life
Now heavy without it.

I remind you of your uncle
The one you put in jail.
The harms committed against you
When you were only a child.

I am that kid again
So powerless
Innocent
Overwhelmed with pleasure.
And still you love her more.

I love fucking you I say
Just so you'll fuck me harder.
Powerless
Innocent
Overwhelmed with pleasure.
It's true
You love her more.

The leaves wither and break
Little bits of me
Wind blown and fallen
To become soil again
The dirt that we are
The two of us.
This passion.
This prison.
And we were only children.

III.X

I knew it would be you. I saw that silly photo of you and I
thought he's next. And you were. Playmates in my playpen.
But more than that, it was my heart that manifested this muddy
pigpen to muck around in. Cold cool earth— the stench of shit
and piss beneath us, our souls trapped in a baffling cycle of
filth. It was fun until it wasn't. We're nice people, or at least I
was until I met you. I thought of her every time we fucked. A
sick pleasure that made me cum again and again. I believed
you. I believed everything.

III.XI

Fisting me made you a man.
I should never have fucked you.
That video of us
Near the water.
Choking me
Like my mother did when I called my father a fag.

I affectionately called it peanut.
Dropped it whole in my mouth.
A crunch and it was gone.
And to partly dignify you
Partly—
I didn't even peal it.

You laughed
But I meant to hurt you.
That peanut, it was yours.
It delighted me
That a man
With so much power
Could have such a small dick.

Hurt you before you hurt me
Leave you before you leave me
But it didn't end there
Half my brain rattled when we spoke.

This spell you cast
Mind torture
It was a game for me
That ended in such torment
Like the skylark
You mock me
Your sin.

III.XII

Born bad
Original sin
I lied when I said that I liked it.
But what was worse?
The lie or the act?

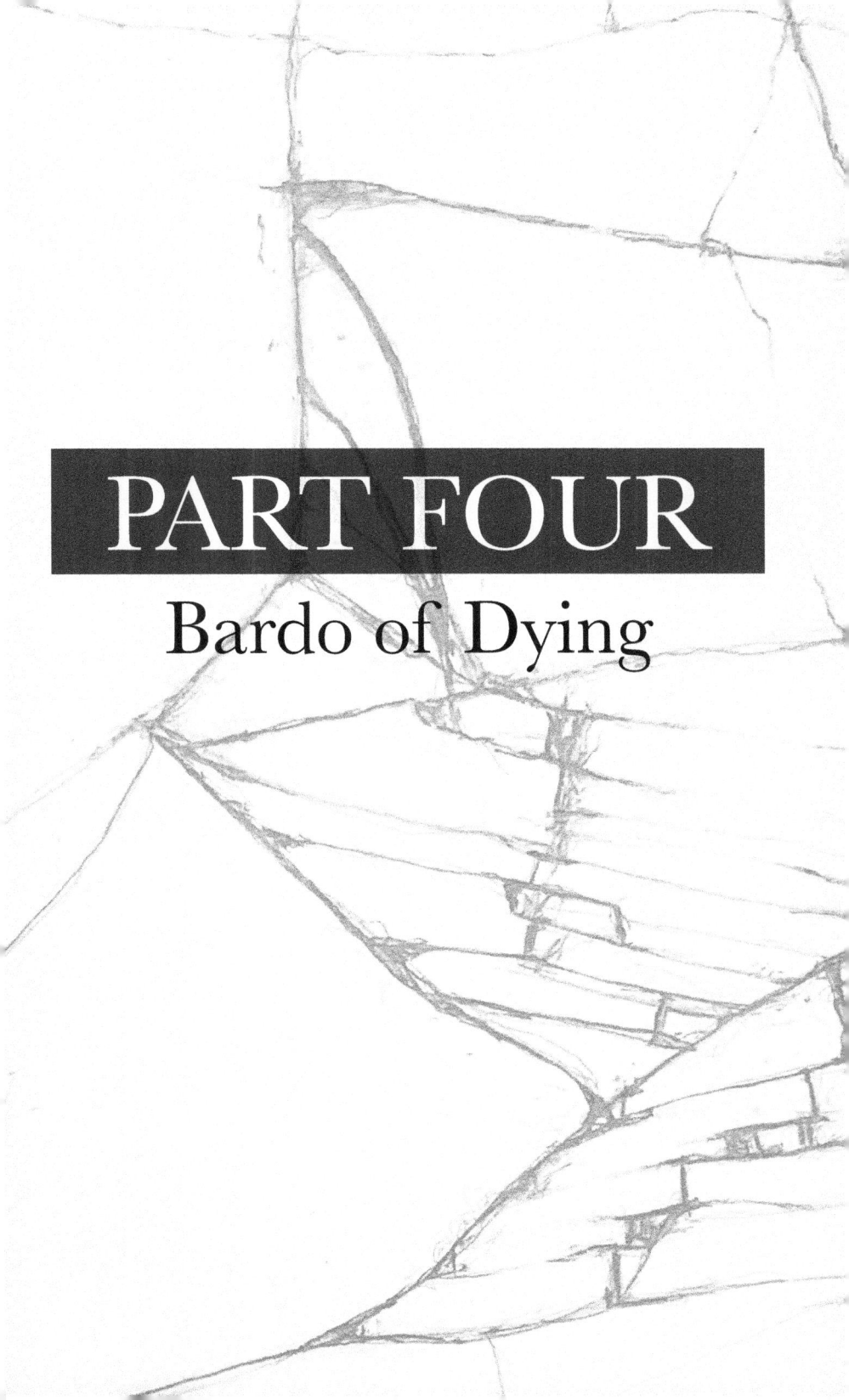

PART FOUR

Bardo of Dying

My lungs will take me
Eventually
In my sixties to seventies
Something in the air will make it impossible for me to breathe
A problem the child will cure
And take us all
And our remains
To Nirvana.

She was there to help my karma along.
I couldn't figure out a way to get the sharps out
The used ones that I injected
Just underneath her skin.
She was sick.
The needles were sick.
I grew sick
The invisible symptoms
Pursued me
Like
My past life courtesan
A lover
Who loved me
As I lay dying.

He was long gone
The Warrior King
Whose blood
Spread through the expanse
Of his imaginary kingdom.
My kingdom was real.
For the empire was mine
Even the air was mine
To breathe in death
As I chose it.

I loved her and she grew sick.
I kept her

Not wanting her to let go.
I was returning the favor
From our past lives.
My love
Who pushed my karma along.
She was mine.
As she lay dying
In my arms
Samsara
Won me
Again.

IV.II

This is the moment
I feared most.
My intuition
Gave you to me.
This premonition
Took you away.
I take shelter
Humbly
Under your golden feet
As we make love.

As we make love
Centuries pass between us.
I've been chasing you
For lifetimes.
To be with you in this way.

At one time your child
A beloved pet another
Your cherished friend
Your mother's sister
Closer and closer

To finally arrive here in bed with you.
The canopy billowing
It's softness touches us
Intermittently
As you adorn me
With lifetimes of tenderness
Bending
Like heated glass—
Sweet baby kisses
The strength of ages.

I cried when we climaxed
Because I knew it would be our last time.
Intuition gave you to me.
This premonition took you away.

What if I told you that we would have other lives together
I say.

I let go
And you live on.
And because I love you

I let go
And you live on.

In forty nine days
I am reborn
My purpose
An undeniable love
A bond unlike any other.
Mother to child
Child to mother
l love you as you love me
Again and again and again.

Nirvana.

IV.III

The Hindus believe
If a demon is murdered
By the merciful hand
Of a god

An incarnation

An avatar

That
Demon
Is instantly released
From Samsara—
And ascends to enlightenment.

That
Demon
Murdered by purity
Is free.

You kill
Because the demons
Are drawn to you
You kill because the demons
Know.

They come for you
And you kill
To release them
From this suffering cycle of life.

The most blessed
The most courageous
The most celebrated
The most worshipped

My heart breaks for you
My darling.
But I am long dead.

IV.IV

They come for you
My darling
But
You
Let intuition guide you
My voice
Now your own.

A sacred dance of language
We speak silently
Timelessly
To one another
One voice.

They blame me
Mass graves and massacres
Don't believe what they say
This prophecy
Is you.

IV.V

It's not easy for you
My darling
They come
And to defend yourself
You take lives.
The weight
On your heart
So unbearable
Like a sitting ghost
Relentlessly
Baring down on your soul.
I gasp
As you gasped
The first time we made love.

IV.VI

Our last words
Fill my breath with tranquility
As I lay dying.
I am gone.
But in my temple
I know you will return.
Some may fear you
But I know who you are.

Siddhartha.

IV.VII

Is it true
That even the demons
Who walk among us
Even those who lead
Or mislead

Could be deities in disguise?
Too terrible to conceive of
But I think it's true
Kali
The goddess of wrath
Brings life to an end
So that humanity might live again.
Lighter this next time
Enlightened the time after that
Until we ascend this cyclical fate.

Is it true
That in this time of Kaliyuga
The demons look just like you?
Like us.

Siddhartha too
In human form
His guns blaze
Armed with centuries of strength
At the firing line.

Siddhartha
Come to save us.
Conquer the half human demons
That we all might ascend this suffering.

Please be with me
The Queen
Keep me safe
In the temple

And let our singular voice
Bleed fire
That evaporates to mist—
This is the prophecy.

IV.VIII

Twin spirits
Soulmates
Fairy brides
In human form
Your karma
Isn't coming for you
It's here to heal you
Sit back
Relax
Clear the way.

IV.IX

The day I got out of the hospital, life changed forever. A
distressed paper bag contained all that was left of me. Three
days worth of pills, a stuffed bunny, and I forget the rest. There
wasn't much else...my beads. The tulsi and the ones I made in
art therapy. The orderlies only let me chant on the real ones if I
sat in solitary confinement. And so I did. The Tibetan Queen
turned psycho or the psycho turned Tibetan Queen. I can't
make sense of it because there isn't any. Or there isn't anymore
sense left in me.

The apartment was the way that I left it. Except, I forget. The mattress was overturned from when I showed the cops the three human skulls. Medication brought new eyes to my body and soul now. Vision impaired, I had almost forgotten that I am the queen. My mind's eye blinded by a layman's disguise. I never wanted to be normal. Or maybe this new normal becomes me. Do you know why you're here? Who's the president? When was the last time that you ate? When was the last time that you slept? The president is me. I don't eat because I'm a pop star. I'm here because it's my karma. I sleep to dream. I dream. I dream. I dream. Please don't ever wake me.

IV.XI

Past life lovers
Not even death can
Break our bond

But you

This

Us

Blinds me

This
Us

Passion
A prison

We've overstayed
Our welcome.

A slight shift
And desire
Leaves humanity in ruins.

We pay the price.
The greatness
That we once were
Becomes nothing.

Sweet bliss
Our curse
Our suffering.

IV.XII

The Kaliyuga Queen
With cursed karma

I changed something
I missed my chance
A second time
I can feel it
Below my heart
In my gut.

The Willful Queen—
But was it my fault
Should I be punished for loving?

What have I done?

Reverse fate
This is my plea
My plight
My petition to christ.
To serve
To right the wrong.

Hear my prayer.

A tiny mis-step
And the entire dance disappears
The past
The future
Suspended.
I am your Queen
Have mercy on me.

IV.XIII

My head heavy with medication, I half think of this line I know
From Chekov…. it's the opening of the play—Uncle Vanya. It's
A nice day, isn't it? Nice day, yes. Nice day to hang yourself. In
My half-slumber on the way to work, I think yes.

It's a nice day indeed.

IV.XIV

The child.

The child
Is his
In this life.
The mother and father
Asian descendants
Identity otherwise unknown.

The child
The one
My past life son.
He despises me.

Everything
Every detail
To become his.
To one day intuit.
A prophet.

Like him
My future
My demise
Information
I didn't ask for
A blessed curse.
My intuition
A portal of power
From which to prepare.

He devises a new way of breathing.
The creator
Of life
Of breath
Of enlightenment.

A civilization
Revived
By one.
My past life son.

IV.XV

The Past Life Queen.
Sullied by self-loathing.
I hate myself for knowing too much.
Information I never asked for.

Please kill the messenger.

IV.XVI

Half my brain rattled. A side effect of the symphony of medication. Here's an idea. That we are all asleep in ignorance until we come to understand the nature of mind. I awoke. Just before I was committed. I woke and I remembered. Queen Búrté, the Mother of Asia— the first Queen of Mongolia. I ran the holy empire while Genghis Khan conquered. The first queen of the largest contiguous empire to this day. Me. I. Queen.

IV.XVII

A life truncated
By fate
Interrupted.
Ignorance drowns me
Like my mother did.
Ignorance
Like quicksand
Pulls me
Away from destiny.
The most blessed person in the world
No more.

One interruption
Caused my world to shift—
My karma.
His karma.
His karma.
Constantly changing.

Cause and effect.

IV.XVIII

I hope
I wake
From this ignorance
In the next life.

As they say:

To know
About your past life
Look to your present
Circumstances.

To know
Your future
Look at your present
Actions.

Cause and effect.

Queen/Hero/Goddess
Kind in this life
To manifest kindness in the next.
This is enlightenment
For all beings.

This is my prayer.

God
If it be thy will
Lighten the heavy load of this life
And take me
Hold me close
I want to be with you.

IV.XIX

A civilization built on blood
And commerce
The Mongol Empire
Was mine
To have and to hold
To love.

Nomadic shaman
Buddhist mystics
Religion no obstacle to
The spiritual mission to overtake the world—
Genghis Kahn
Abroad and beyond
The master strategist of
Warfare and terror
Found no war
Between us
He and I
At our dwelling place.

Goddess Queen and advisor
I counseled on all things
Natural to our survival.
The Silk Road
Currency
A radical system of capital.
A practical system of diplomacy.
All with a refined sense of love
And power.
The Mother of Asia.

My father
His Holiness
A spiritual guide and keeper
Soul secrets
Clues to the kingdom
That was Timujin
The Great Kahn.

As I search for my conspirators
Lifetime after lifetime
After lifetime
After lifetime
Each life passing
Our karmic debt more evident.

We/he
He/they
Missing/found
The Masters of Kaliyuga
The progenitors of pain and civil savagery
Have left behind a legacy of violence
Of capital
Of commerce
That humanity must bleed out.

My darlings
Wake from your slumber of ignorance
It is time to pay.

IV.XX

What if I told you that I know. Long before the act. Nomadic
shaman. Buddhist mystics. Rulers of the future. Our mission to
conquer the world. To dominate, procreate, master. Create a
new legacy. And we succeed as we did then. To right the
wrong(s) of our past transgressions. Blessed and cursed to
survive and to lead once again. A new civilization this time. Built
on the light that we are. And love. They call me crazy but I
know. I've been told. The singer, her brother. The poet rappers.
The orator. The holy ones and those of us who conquer. I lead
with compassion this time. Complicit, all of us. Past life
accomplices to the crime that is love. We manifest love in this
life, in the time of suffering— Kaliyuga. This is the prophecy. I
am crazy but don't kill me, not yet. I am the messenger.

IV.XXI

The Willful Queen.
Kaliyuga
A material body
A lifetime wasted.
A gesture of greed.

Siddhartha
My love.
His purity
My ultimate desire

Unbearable

Past life queen to king
Siddhartha
The ruler of my world.
A love with the strength of ages
Though not strong enough for this life.

The universe is love
And yet
Karma
Cause and effect
A paradox too cruel to fathom.

IV.XXII

It was moha I thought. Delusion so powerful it speaks in one's own voice. I wandered the city for forty-nine days. On the forty-ninth day, as I lay dreaming, I followed the white cat of the child me up to the roof to my liberation. The karmic jump that took my breath away. My lungs imploding upon impact. I couldn't fly but my death was blameless. The most blessed Goddess Queen, detached from the mind prison of their suffering. Dying all the time. This is life. Perhaps my present actions will put me back on my destined path. The next moment my next life. The moment after that, my next death. This is my prayer as my soul soars into clear light.

PART FIVE

Bardo of Luminous Dharmata—The Intrinsic Nature of Everything

V.I

Luminosity—

Our next leader

American

Something else

Or

Something having to do with hollywood (?)

Neither female
Nor male.

Our next leader
Is not
But is.

A mystic.

Our next leader
Blessed
And highly favored.

Clear light.

Our next leader
Will have had a hard life.

So as
To know
To remember
To know—
To break the curse
And expunge the unthinkable woes
Of the

Corrupt
From humanity.

Our next leader
Will sleep in ignorance
Only to wake
Holy and
Whole.
Steering us on course
To our next destiny.

VII

Hollywood (?) A film about Tibet and it's lost Queen. My next life destiny. The Tibetan Embassy will find me. My next life destiny, a crown to free me. My past life debt to repay. To help humanity out of the cycle of suffering. To help humanity out of the cycle of violence and commerce, the past life legacy of Búrté and Timujin. Of queen…and king. The mother and father of Asia.

V.III

Roll sound
Roll camera
The film (I)
Mark:

A girl pursued by illusion.
A Tibetan monk
A guardian spirit
Turned menace
Pursuing me
Like my past life karma—
My unpaid debt.
Memory
A light
To centuries past
A luminous guide to my freedom.
The Queen
A delusion
Turned fact
Maybe
Fact
Fact
Fact.

V.IV

A single flame
To light the way
Because it's dark where you might be.
A cup of water
For clarity
To end your confusion.
An offering of snacks
To assuage your hunger.
Empowered by the strength of my ancestors
Of my higher good
A sacred chant
For your enlightenment

Om
Mani
Padme
Hung

I say

Let go
Let go
Let go.

V.V

Rolling rolling
Slate in
The film (II)
Mark:

The Queen.
A mystic with the wrong chant.
Waitress by day.
Exorcist by night.
False self.

The dead need help.
The witch's uncrossing
A mystic queen with the wrong spell.
Ego.
False perception of self.

V.VI

The camera is rolling
The film (III)
Mark:

The dead need help.

Timujin/Búrté
Save us again.
Past life lovers
Two souls
Centuries strong
Entwined again is this life.

A film in a film
About a queen
And their king
Repaying a past life debt.

Tulkus reunited with their reigning kingdom
Lifetimes past
An empire of memories
Restored like salt to an ocean wave
So as to govern again.

Tibet
Tibet
Tibet

Clear light.

V.VII

The intrinsic nature of everything.
The space between the past and future
Reveals self-radiance
Clear light

Being still ignorant to rigpa
To the landscape of light
The phases of the
Luminous Dharmata
Unfold
As they do
Each time I fail to recognize them.

A body of light
Sound
Light
Color

As wisdom
Unites—
Deities dissolve
Into me

Till finally:

All accomplishing wisdom
A portent yet to appear

Arriving to:

The limitless clairvoyance
Of the space/time continuum.

V.VIII

Public Address (or a part of it)

If you witness a crime and do nothing, you are complicit. By doing nothing you become an accomplice. The crime is yours too. This is spiritual bankruptcy. A crime we are all guilty of. This affliction is global and it's ours for our children to inherit if we do nothing. This is the prophecy. Call me Queen. Call me the messenger. Kill me, I'm dying everyday.

V.IX

The initiation was just as the ancestors told me it would be.
Spirits danced with the monks all night scaring me senseless
with moans-whispers-rattles. The largest monk held what felt
like a door onto to my much smaller frame, sitting on me,
stealing my breath as sitting ghosts do. Other monks grabbed
at me. Blew on my body until my hairs stood upright. I called
upon my ancestors of the highest good to guide me, to all the
powers of good in the universe, to the greatest good within me
and my chant, my mantra rose to my lips: om mani padme
hung I repeated— a prayer for protection, a petition for
enlightenment for all beings. In the morning, one of the monks
asked how I slept. I was to respond very well thank you. Three
nights of this horror-show terrified and beguiled me. How did
you sleep? I was asked. Very well thank you.

V.X

As the world watches
With watering eyes
Tibet in Exile
Now Tibet
Redefined.

Old power
With the strength of ages.

The Queen.
Their King.
Govern/Conquer.
Nonviolence their new code.
Wisdom that realizes egolessness.

Lost for centuries.
New power
Once in exile
Now restored.

The world watches
With watering eyes
Tibet in Exile
Now Tibet
Redefined.

Public Address (or another part of it)

I am the Queen of Tibet, identified as the reincarnation of the ancient Queen, Queen Búrté Katan; the first Queen of Mongolia, the wife of Timujin— otherwise known as the great Genghis Kahn. Rulers of Asia around the turn of the thirteenth century, Búrté ran the empire while Genghis Kahn conquered. Eventually the two became the leaders of the largest contiguous empire known to this day. Their contribution to civilization was vast, creating a culturally sustainable infrastructure, with a particular brilliance in diplomacy, art, and commerce. The dominant strength of their formidable empire was war; Genghis Kahn, a brilliant military strategist employed the use of gunpowder for the first time, perfected an ambush of terror, and used a 'survival of the fittest" system of colonization upon each territory he invaded. Influenced by Nomadic Shamanism and Buddhist Mysticism, Genghis Kahn's mission was spiritual, believing that he was led to victory under every circumstance in the name of god as he understood it. The daughter of Genghis Kahn's spiritual advisor, I believe that I've chosen my rebirth to repay a karmic debt to humanity. commerce and war, as instituted by my past life empire, pervasive to this day, are the two factors, I believe, that will be responsible for the eventual demise of civilization as we are living it. And this is why my soul has chosen Tibet. Contrary to the Mongol Empire of my past life, Tibet is governed politically by the Buddhist philosophies of compassion and nonviolence. Guests of India until Tibet is freed, we find our strength in our Buddhist tradition. Although we are a nation of immense spiritual strength we are materially detached and as a result economically poor. We are currently sustained through the generosity of the Indian and American governments and we are most grateful. As the new leader of the most spiritual nation in the world I would like to propose a revolutionary idea: that currency, as well, can be spiritual. My aim as the Queen of Tibet in Exile is to create a financially stable economy, financially self-sustaining economy. At the moment, we are incapable of financial solvency, although in a short time I plan to be. A tithe is what I like to call the "Currency of the Spirit". My petition to those who are able is a monthly tithe of 1% of their income, a spiritual act of kindness in support of Tibet in Exile until we are financially self-supporting. Once our schools, monasteries, and hospitals are in place, when the needs of every Tibetan in Exile are met, I feel it will be our turn to give tithings to other nations less fortunate. It would be our honor to pay your tithings forward— and this is how we globally heal. This is love and compassion. This is living with spiritual dignity. This is Buddhism. And this is Tibet.

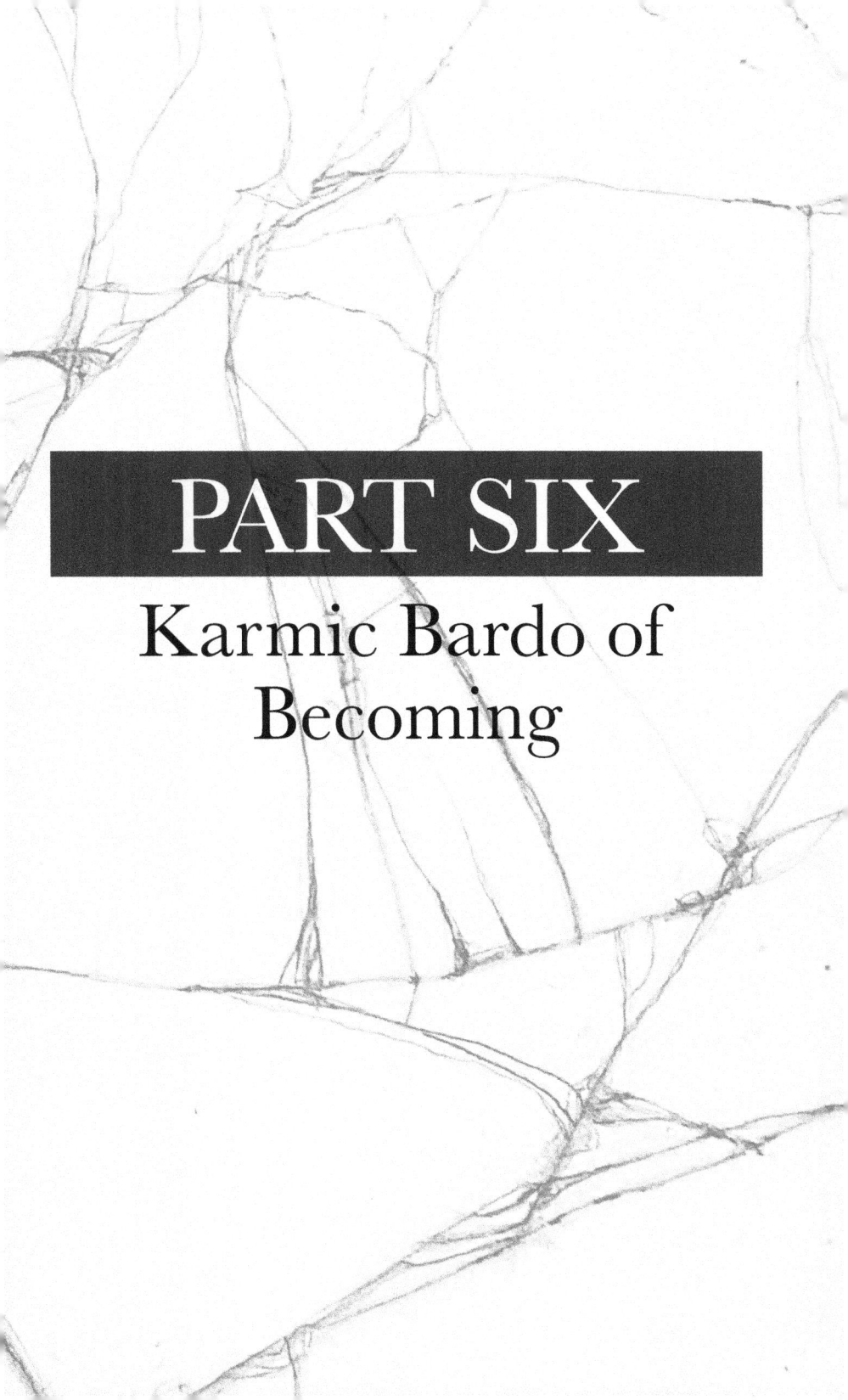

PART SIX

Karmic Bardo of Becoming

VI.I

Last night I lay dying as I slept
Floating there
In the in-between space
Involuntarily rigid
Nearly conscious
Nearly a corpse.
I held in my breath
And let out a rattling moan—
A moan equally full of fear
As desire.
My time was nearing the end.
On the trail to Mount Everest
Pulled along
In the last car of
The nomadic caravan
My then world painted
In grey and blues.

I woke from the nightmare
Centuries later.

I don't want to hold you back I say
The smoke of war
Burning in my lungs.
The burden of the future
Too thick to inhale.
I'm sick
With information I never asked for.
The prophecy now manifest
Everlasting fire too soon to consume us.

I close my eyes tight
Blinded by the sight of him in my mind's eye.
A vision so evil
My entire body weakens
From the pressure
Of perfect grief.

They come for us
Day and night.
Relentlessly savage
The years of deprivation
Starvation
The years of abandonment
The years of hell
Fill our once peaceful world
With hungry ghosts.

Stepping over blood and bones
We travel on foot
Almost seven-hundred miles
From Dharamsala to Tibet
The quiet
So vast at times
It chills my pure soul
Into tiny
Rancid bits
Even the devil
Dares not consume.

My past life destiny
Wars with me.
A nomadic holy kingdom
Lost again
On a steep winding
Mountain trail.

My past life intuition at work
I want to forget
I remember
I forget again.

The second largest contiguous empire
Known to this day
Stolen three times in a row.
On the fourth turn

The thief
The demon dictator
The demoniac force
Behind the crime
Usurps the throne.
The second largest
Now becomes the largest.
An empire stolen.

On the path to the peak
Advanced in my years now
My material body
A mismatch
For the strength of my subtle body.
I've taken a shot to my thigh.
The flesh broken and bloody
An infection oozes through the skin
Where the bullet was lodged
Up to the surface.

The Warrior King
With the strength of ages
Refuses to leave me behind.
I want to let go I say
Please go on without me.
I show the poison
I've packed with me
Knowing
That this moment would come.
Our karma merges
You and I my King
As I am pulled
My body
Heavy with injury
Over your shoulder
You tie me to your back.

Centuries strong
You repay a karmic debt

to me.
An unbearable weight
Your material body
Laden with conquering strength
But I would not relent.
Eleven centuries ago
I carried you.

And today
The one
The boy
Our past life son
Now grown
Is with us.
His wife
The orator's daughter too.
We've brought the cure of the disease with us
Although it has yet to be unearthed.
The boy is close.
When the holy palace is overtaken
The pursuers breech our inner wall.
A born strategist
The King
You move us on.

The climb
The cold
The ice
Oh my darling I say
Leave me behind—
Then follow me to the next life.
Chase me as I chase you
But let me go.

At the next landing
We take shelter in a cave.
My disease-ridden lungs broken now
You build a pyre
No poison

My decision is natural.
The most enlightened moment of life
Is mine now.
I let go and god is merciful.
I love you
My King.

I've been here before.
I recognize it.
My mental body
Breaks through the ground
Breaks through the ordinary mind.
Luminosities merge
To the nature of mind
Insight restored
To omniscience—
To the enlightened mind.

Free of desire
Anger
Jealousy
And ignorance
Realizing that none
Of these are real—
I rest in this empty nature
As the winds of karma
Pass before me.
My practice
In the Bardo of Living
Closes the entrance to another
Rebirth.
I am reborn in the Buddha realm.

After three days
My material body
Is wrapped
And left behind
For the vultures.
The sky my burial now.

You detach from me
The memory of me
For holding on could
Risk my passing
To my next destiny.
I love you
My King
I love you
I love you.

Without emotion or ego
You and the boy
You and the camp move on.
An avalanche nearly overtakes you.
But you are determined.
The challenge means nothing to you.

At last arriving to the top
Pursued by sorrow
You mourn for me.
I love you
My King.
I love you.

In the years to come
You build another empire.
As the boy works on the cure
Your civilization thrives.
In twenty years time
Knowing this prophecy
You wait.
Reunited once more
I am reborn.
In twenty years time my love
You call me child.
The boy and his wife
My chosen parents this time—
The cure procured at last.
A civilization on the path to enlightenment

At long last
Kaliyuga has run its course.
I am reborn to bathe you
In my love I say.
You let go
And I am here with you.
I am Queen again.
I am Búrté.

AUTHOR'S NOTE

I have been hearing voices since I was a child. My favorite voice is WIm, the voice of my wiser self or wise mind. In times of crisis, she comforts me with details of my future. I named her WIm and she consented. The letter "I" in her name is intentionally capitalized because her voice is for me, about me and no one else can hear her. She even speaks like me but softer, with more breath and nasality. I began a practice of notating what WIm tells me during my last hospitalization. 15 years later, what began in orange crayon at Bellevue Psychiatric, has resulted in my book, *The Tenderness of Glass*.

Part memoir and part manifesto, *The Tenderness of Glass* is a non-traditional book of narrative verse and prose poetry. Each of my book's six parts are named after a Tibetan Buddhist Bardo. Beginning with the "Bardo of Life," we follow the Goddess Palden Lhamo through the underworld to her next chosen body. The body she chooses is me— transgender and native of the Pacific Islands, raised with abuse in the United States.

In the the "Bardo of Dreams" we enter the psychiatric hospital; a world where the spirit is distorted by heavy medication. Having "fallen out of love with life," the narrative is pushed by love and loving in the "Bardo of Meditation." From love comes the inspired "Bardo of Dying "where the reincarnation of the Goddess takes form in the many lives of Queen Búrté. Spiritual luminosity restores the Queen to their rightful throne as the Queen of Tibet. The last part of my book, "The Bardo of Becoming," is a vision for the destruction of an apocalyptic future. From the wrath of this destruction, humanity is led to a new nirvana..

—Jodi Lin

SPECIAL THANKS

There are many treasured advisors I want to thank. Of the following list, many live and breathe in the realm of the living. Some have moved on.

My Ancestors of the Seediq Tribe
Palden Lhamo
Padmasambhava
Avilokiteshvara
Mahakala
All the Buddhas and Bodhisattvas of the past present,
future, and beyond
Ar Yen
Janice Lin
Peter Lin
Denise Bell
Julian Talamantez Brolaski
Jan Schmidt and Arthur Rivers
Ocean and Stu Yen Chuang Mathews
Helen and Kristy Lin Billuni
Esther Wang

ABOUT JODI

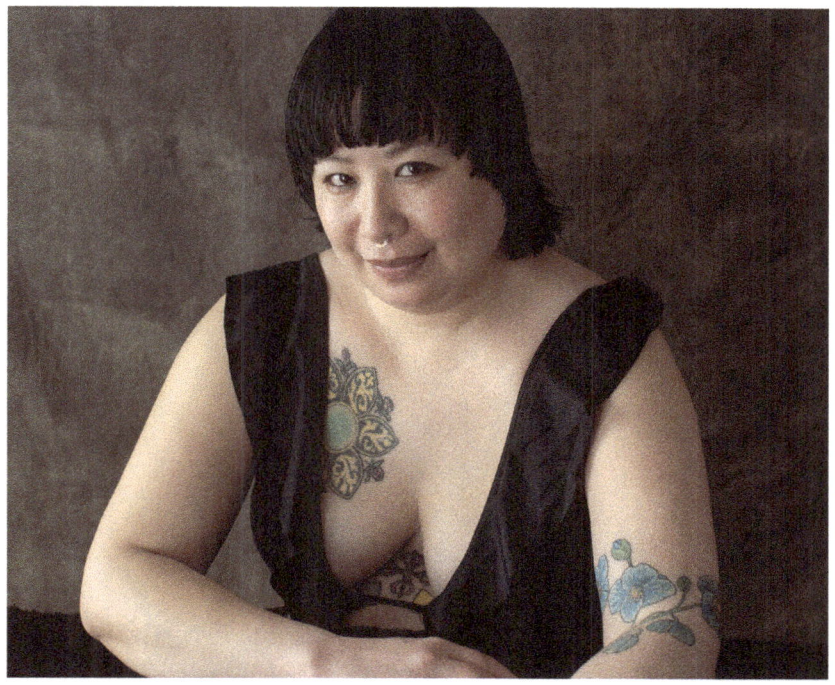

photo by Brett Lindell

Jodi Lin identifies as a gender-expansive poet, filmmaker and a person who hears voices. Taiwanese of the Seediq Tribe, they are currently based in Manhattan. Their poetry can be experienced in a video diary called *Leaving Beauty* on YouTube, *Open Fruit Magazine*, *Amethyst Review*, Poetry Project's *Footnotes* and others. Graduate of the ART Institute at Harvard, Sarah Lawrence College and a Brooklyn Poets Fellow. Their short film, *Borte, Queen of Tibet* was nominated for the festival prize at Soho International Film Festival and received numerous other screenings. Their writing practice is enriched by the certified peer recovery coaching and support they provide. *The Tenderness of Glass* is their debut collection from new words {press}.The book was written as an offering of a new world to their ancestors.

ABOUT NW{P}

new words {press} is a non-profit poetry press publishing trans* & gender-expansive poets & hybrid writers.

support our efforts & the incredible writers we publish. visit us at **newwordspress.com**